other books by Amrita Skye Blaine

poetry:
forthcoming from Finishing Line Press mid-2025:
every riven thing

other books by Skye Blaine

memoir:
Bound to Love, a memoir of grit and gratitude

fiction:
The Pensing Connection trilogy:
Book 1: *Unleashed*
Book 2: *Must Like Dogs*
Book 3: *Passing the Torch*

strange grace

the ending season

Amrita Skye Blaine

Copyright © 2025 Amrita Skye Blaine

All rights reserved. No part of this publication may be reproduced or transmitted in any form or by any means, electronic, mechanical, magnetic, photographic including photocopying, recording or by any information storage and retrieval system, without prior written permission of the publisher. No patent liability is assumed with respect to the use of the information contained herein. Although every precaution has been taken in the preparation of this book, the publisher and author assume no responsibility for errors or omissions. Neither is any liability assumed for damages resulting from the use of the information contained herein.

ISBN: 979-8-9923023-0-1
Published by:
    Berkana Publications
    Sebastopol CA 95472 USA

Author's websites and contact information:
    www.theheartofthematter-dailyreminders.org
    www.skyeblaine.com
    amritaskyepoetry@gmail.com

Cover image: photo by Amrita Skye Blaine
Other interior photos: http://www.depositphotos.com

Printed in the United States of America

*to the one truth
that holds us all*

*Absence my presence is,
strangeness my grace*

—*Cælica* by Fulke Greville [1554-1628]
sonnet LXIX

Table of Contents

velvet now 7

the way

surfing the curl 10
terminal 11
remember your death 12
skins 13
due at the bank 14
the deal 15
ebb and flow 16
domino rollercoaster 17
bone house 18
fragrance 19
bewilderment and tenacity 20
our world 21
gravity 22
dying away 23
I am dust and divinity 24
in the road 25
the welcome 26
sweet danger 27
the score 28
the shift 29

close connections

diverted 33
I remember 34
case study 36
why? 37
grieving advice 38
slip on the world 39

on the way 40
lurker 41
scanning 42
where 43
another loss 44
regret 45
leaving 46
passing away 47
gone not gone 48
after the dying 49

the ending season

entering late life 53
ghosts 54
the age of loss 55
late-blooming flower 56
come home 57
alone 58
road signs 59
losing 60
event horizon 61
the demand 62
timebound 63
adsum 64
metronome 65
wild ride 66
the leaving times 68
days 69
everyday new 70
breaking 71
trees sway 72
surrender 73
fall into astonishment 74

reflection	75
that kind	76
the waiting times	77
lifted	78
give way	79
good fortune	80
laid spare	81
dancing the loss	82
past due	83
leaving it all	84
looking ahead	85
the shift	86
the score	87
slow learner	88
borrowed	89
the wish	90
Acknowledgements	93
Poet's bio	95

velvet now

So keep this refuge in mind—the back roads of yourself.
—Marcus Aurelius

the day so thick
sit
sit at the edge
the edge of
a glen
shuck off shoes
wiggle your toes
one slow breath
and mind empties

soft wind clears
doubt
air freshens
worries coast

step out on foot
roads trail off
soon gravel, soon
dirt, soon slender
paths   yours
yours

the way

surfing the curl

the wave
curls above

body puny
within
bare feet grip
the board
mind
empties

ocean roars
slicing water

only this

ride the current
or fall hard

terminal

I'm leaving—
leaving
the instant I arrive
you are, too
that's the deal

we get magnolias
in flamboyant bloom
love so strong
it flays us wide

we get plagues
and headaches
puzzles to solve
feuds and famine
the breadth of it all

yet also light
luminous ground
radiating   ineffable
pulsing from the core
grab my hand
let's stay for the ride

remember your death

every thing returns
home
no choice

blue whale and
smallest shrew
all have allotted
span—you do too

earthbound
time—precious
and doesn't matter
even stars sputter out

arrival and leavetaking—
can you celebrate
coming home?

skins

first, shaping skins
to blend
family and world
baffling
compulsory
attempting to fit
not   and not

shedding begins
toddle out of babyhood
wrenched from home
daycare
school to work
on and on

each skin
a shucking
betraying new beneath

and then   and then

due at the bank

fingers intertwined
sun warm on
my back

slaking my thirst
the sweet-tart taste
of fresh-squeezed juice

splashing cool
stream water
on my face after
an autumn hike

the first, rich
scent of rain
on parched ground

my precious body
one-and-only

all of it
all on loan

the deal

The pain I feel now is the happiness I had before.
That's the deal. —C. S. Lewis

that hawk, coasting
he dips to one side,
his wings just so, to catch
the shifting air   I stand
and stare, the fugitive
moment

there was a time,
caught in my own
self-importance, too
busy to soak in what's
fleeting   now as I grow
old and absorb all
will be lost, snapshots
of grace are salve
and consolation
not to be overlooked
or wasted

ebb and flow

waves thunder in,
recede to the sea
gusts of rain
wash over, pass through
hearts empty and fill
100,000 beats a day

we come, we go—
some young, some old
more swiftly than
we can envision—
how to bear the flow
of inexorable rhythm?

domino rollercoaster

glancing at news
line them up just so
touch the first,
and tick tick tick
familiar icons grown
up with gone,
one, next, another
knocked down, a slow-
motion river
now some days
more than one
so it is with friends—
lifesuit no longer
needed, left behind
us, too

bone house

some days I think
about all the bones
in this batty bone house
called earth—my calculator
coughs counting bones
eight billion of us
living now, 206 bones
in each, much less
bat and bird bones
the trillions of fish bones—
an invention
that apparently serves
but where do they go?
they dissolve
into love and dust
nourish the ground
for what's next

fragrance

Is not impermanence the very fragrance of our days?
—Rainer Maria Rilke

first rain
thirsty land
petrichor bouquet
earthy spice
here   soon gone

we hunger
for what vanishes
the very losing
cue and call
reminding
life so fleeting,
perfume fades

clinging doesn't serve

bewilderment and tenacity

I watch the sparrows bathe
how they dip and shake
the bevy of doves grazing
the ground for seeds

at the marrow, life is raw
it takes starch and love
resolve and guts
and bundles of kindness

this has been my path
bewilderment and tenacity —
wonder and shock at
the ways of the world
the grit to bear down
and bear with

the birds know how to be —
relaxing, I know, too

our world

Oh, to love what is lovely and will not last!
—Mary Oliver

different timeline
but transient,
our tender world,
bound for loss
just like us

sun and cluster
further behind
nonetheless, will die
sucked
into black holes
or blazing balls

all this loveliness
making way
for what's next

gravity

not consequence
but weight—the
pull that tethers
me to ground

I don't bemoan the
toll—bent
back and sagging face—
even as earth
drags me to her,
gravity is both
dogged and required

noting the gifts,
feet stay planted
on the ground   the sun
my sustenance
holds earth
at a life-giving distance
and rivers run downhill
so much provided—I
am beholden to gravity

dying away

every moment
one breath
closer to death
the sun, the moon
even our very own
earth, sources
of sustenance
wither, fade
and ebb away

it's the way of things

and yet
it's hard to hold—
the universe
itself grows, ages
and dies—
my mind, a denier
even with evidence
doesn't want to accept

this source of suffering
starts with belief
in past and future
instead of resting
in the cradle of now
let puzzles go
let tension go
now breathes

I am dust and divinity

made of exploding stars
and light, bright
awareness
a paradox at best

divinity births dust
forges a form
breathes planets
and star clusters
amoebas and bacteria
four-leggeds and us

I live in this form awhile
taste blessings
bear grief
smell jasmine
and kiss soft lips
all holy
all part of this mire

I'm shaped to live
this earthly life—
given a circumstance
not of my choosing
then taken back
who knows when

remember, dear one—
lotuses are nourished
in the muck

in the road

Highway 5
south of Redding
a seagull full of life
wheeling in the sky
misjudges   smashing
into a semi's side—
now a broken thing
feathers torn loose
life knocked away
it drops
to the pavement,
there, then gone
so swift a death

barreling along
I tremble,
steady the wheel
notice
my thickening throat
late spring
innocent bird
unwitting trucker
I pray the gull
leaves no starving chicks
and consider
the circle—

ten years ago
and I remember

the welcome

when frailty came
and they could
no longer hunt
native peoples
understood
they walked alone
into wildness
lay down   prayed
and waited
welcoming

animals, too
may slip off solo

what is this need
to cling?
hospital alarms
field days of drugs
and a lifetime of savings
won't protect you

when the body
is done   it's done
slip out of
your earthsuit
a cicada shell—
and fly

sweet danger

There is a sweet danger brewing, and there are no lifeboats.
—Rosemerry Wahtola Trommer

the house finch
splashes, water
warmed by noonday
rays   in her bathing,
neglects to scan—
the heat-seeking missile
nabs with claws, nails her
with beak
the raptor ferries
her away   finch
into red-tail

I want to avert
my gaze   yet this,
our beautiful blue
planet's way
it's not sad
it simply is

the score

if I listen
behind sound
and into silence
it is here—
my inner song

not more or less,
yet unlike yours—
every one of us
called forth
from being

when I study
the score,
entwined motifs
threading movements
some minor
others major
the themes rise—
more solace
more patience

what revelation
the coda brings

the shift

in this ending season,
whether given one
minute or twenty years
my work is clear
the shift from doing
to being—
a poem a day is
doing, no doubt
but this doing
is different,
slowed down
reflective
appropriate to
the season

I will write
until I cannot
praying
that day's
far off

close connections

diverted
1978

on a Delta flight—
how many times I've
imagined—he grabs
his chest, maybe half-
rises, moans or cries
out   his seatmate pounds
the button for help,
hollers *this man needs
a doctor*

a big man slumping,
unconscious, pilot called,
plane diverted
word spreads | cabin's abuzz
muttered complaints of
missed meetings | space
so tight he's laid
in the aisle | no room
to maneuver | attendants
give oxygen | struggle with
CPR   hover—

after landing, their relief
handing him off
to paramedics
Dad doesn't survive

I remember

1978

I remember visiting home
Mom wielding my father's huge car
my son's first time at the zoo

I remember him bouncing the stroller
his rapture at seeing big cats   rush
of stuttering words

I remember the tinny loudspeaker
Mrs. Blaine, to the white kiosk
I remember her turn,
meeting my gaze, her stare

I remember she picked up the phone
her straight back
Mrs. Blaine speaking
I remember color fleeing her face
the bow of her head
then, *your father is dead*

I remember stumbling to the car
my screaming, kicking toddler
who didn't understand
I remember the weight
shrunken mom on my arm
you drive, she said
I remember maneuvering the monster
through a Cincinnati no longer
my own

I remember pitching
the p & j sandwich into my son's lap
anything to silence
his screeches

I remember my mother
I can't wait to tell your fa…
I remember her shock
but no tears

case study

My father came home in a briefcase. Mom plodded toward the wingtip reading chairs, lowering herself into the larger one, a caress for upholstered arms.

The case lonely on the entry slate, unsure, it just looked wrong. Slender. Small. I wanted to hug it close, snap the cool clasps open, see what ashes really meant. Or fling it away, denying.

Dad, sixty-four, Delta flight dead. Hope of a friendship flew with him. Three days later, sultry summer—the burying—not the case, though the urn's color, size, shape, it all escapes.

Where is it—does it have a life after carrying one? Forty-six years on, it summons my father—large, stocky, parachute-white wavy hair, striding, that very briefcase in hand.

why?
1978

please time stop
to honor
this being, both here
and gone

the forging
propulsion
onward, onward
no marking the change
from body to bodiless

this crater that cannot
be filled

grieving advice

thank you, no.
no advice.
this is mine
in the only way
I uncover
each moment
that I can

kintsugi, mending
myself with liquid
gold, love brushed
in the fissures
you left in leaving
evermore apparent
for I am changed

slip on the world

first light
outline of firs
bold against dawn's
soft apricot
I lie in the dark
blink
come to slowly

read the news
of my tribe
death in the family
again—
when did I
start scanning
for losses?
breathe in, allow
grief to enter
my bones

on the way
for Marisa

headed to snip canna lilies
she'd tended with joy,
on her garden path
she dropped—
dead in the dropping
or dying more slowly
she lay in sunshine
staring at blossoms
seeing or not seeing
but I imagine her glad
to fall alone, her space
in the blooming

lurker

she's coming
I feel her lurking
tapping family, friends
and well-known icons
one by one
without exemption

who does the choosing?
and why her jaunty hat?

some slide out easy
others rise to fight
stave her off awhile
but she'll be back,
that one—
she's visited my friend
three times
this time for good

scanning

I'm watching now
close observation

have I lost
something today
I can't retrieve
ever

skill
capacity
or strength
gone for good?
wave goodbye

in time,
I will have to let it go
we all shall, one day

where

fresh mound on the hill—
dog hunts for her friend,
sets a long nose on my leg
her eyes begging *where*

I walk her up to the grave
lie together on the grass
impossible sun glazing
and in a soft tone, explain
Bodhi was sick and suffering
he's no longer in pain

she ponders the hillock
stretches a paw
toward that ground
then shifts to consider me
and there we meet
two sorrowings

another loss

today, another dear friend
gone   we're packing up
one by one
heading for our
truest home
no place, not here
not there

losing so few early on
I knew this day
would come, felt it
in the offing
the tsunami has begun

regret
for Gail

phone pressed
thick throat boulder
listening—
her husband's voice
instead
thin autumn sun
doesn't warm
my friend
is dead

daylong mid-August
road trip   I passed
nearby their home
didn't stop   didn't call—
let weeks months slide

I married them
and no goodbye,
subtle rustlings
inside

leaving

your decision to leave—
not terminal,
you couldn't use the law
so you stopped
eating and drinking
two hard weeks
he said, *two weeks*
it took her to die,
he sounded worn
    worn thin
    worn down
    worn out
trying to imagine
his life
after upholding
your choice

passing away

my life, partner, pup
and my son will all
pass away

we are passing away—
each moment
lost to the next
never to return
but through memory

where kindness
and sorrow reside
we draw close
to what's lost
yet can't touch it

even that recall
changes   fades
disappears

gone not gone

my friend is dead,
right in the center
of my chest—
no reaching out
to touch her, true
yet something
tangible here

my father, too
gone forty-six years
when I attend,
his presence, near

this riddle,
gone not gone
frequents, a trace,
who they are
come close,
dusting

after the dying
in honor of my brother-in-law

one moment
substantial, corporeal
the next,
do you feel the flight
the shift
from their body
to your heart?
a potent change

the body reels
at the reshaping
the loss immense
yet they are here
their love
in the center
of your chest
a firefly of light

grief, an aroma
of love
you can no longer
reach out,
touch them

and yet

the ending season

entering late life

parsing
gleaning
releasing
another passage
different, this phase
all of it inside
there's still work
to be done

ghosts

so sure   and yet
all those
I did not become—
ghosts, my other
selves
veterinarian,
the big one

pictured a lifelong
happy union
got there   but
it took four
yes, marriages

you're barren
the doctor declared
I wasn't ...
surprise!
an imagined life,
the arts, replaced
with a cherished creation

no haunting
and yet
I feel them   even
hear them
we bump shoulders
in the market
these women
I might have been

the age of loss

every day a new reminder
an ache, twinge
a minuscule shift,
but there—
harbinger
marking a different time
saying come
grow   go

a friend reported
my brother died
I'm the last one standing
her gaze a grief
and comprehension

before, a distant veil
floating our way
now here
raw
obdurate
inevitable
the clouds pile—
how majestic they are

late-blooming flower

you're a late bloomer
followed by a sigh
mom's prognosis
in my early years

a storm of inspiration
in my downstream decades
did she see what is true,
or in saying, make it so?

like Mexican bush sage
hundreds of soft
purple fronds
with tiny white flowers
blossoming near winter
I, too, am a riot
of ingenuity and color
blooming late,
blooming long

come home

in slanted sunshine
I close my eyes   rest
eavesdrop as birds
tuck in for night

noticing, as I elder
into old,
calls me home

in autumn's harvest,
how to put it all to bed?
kindness, gratitude
fruit my shortening days

alone

birthed alone
dying our own
even with family
nearby

solitary feelings
even as I love
I cannot know

road signs

*slow down   sharp
corners ahead*
the age of unexpected
turns for myself
and others
when the phone
rings at odd hours
who now?

losing

the art of losing isn't hard to master —Elizabeth Bishop

our childhood dog
then our youth
our innocence
all will go—
loss of dreams
first love

children grown
parents gone
friends picked off
then slow decline
what isn't hard to master?

watch for nightfall
lie in the field, allow
the canopy of stars
to soak you
it all comes down to this

beneath the losses
something rests
steady and bright
it can't be found
cannot be touched
yet holds us

event horizon

I see death now
easing up
over the horizon
sauntering my way
probably not today
maybe not tomorrow

perhaps fifteen
likely less
I can't know
do I want to know,
have the courage to know?

the demand

this, life's demand
I bear the surprise

choice carries weight
I'm seventy-eight
bent by its pull

timebound

clothed in a body
and a point of view
as much as I deny
make up stories
cry out against
the inevitable end

my body, the view
I hold so precious
only temporary

bound for loss
everything comes and goes
that's how it has to be

or the cosmos
would overbrim
everything includes
a motley crew of humans
who have to go, too
recycling is required

adsum

a fragile life form
drying out
here   right now
knowing this
a humbling

what to do
the next breath
and smile

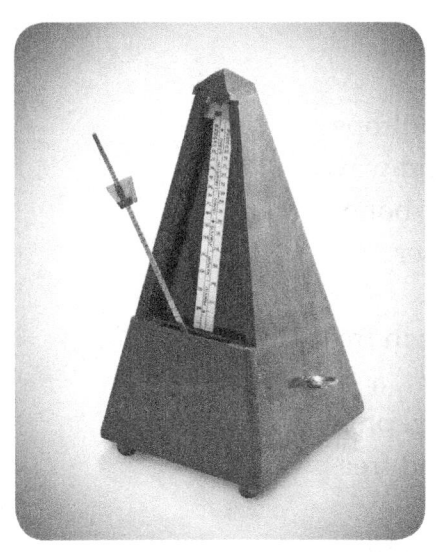

metronome

the polished mahogany
case on the Baldwin
baby grand, tick tick
back and forth
the tempo I labored
to match playing
Hanon scales again
again, again

now, my habitual heart-
beat, a living metronome
with lifelong sporadic
syncopation   each
evening I give thanks
its cadence,
counting down
the days

wild ride

dips and hilltops
troughs and waves
a skin-and-bone
rollercoaster
this life
sometimes in free fall—
it can buffet, a sideways
bluster or zephyr
delicate and free

rarely tranquil

when days roll by—
writing flows, friends
thrive, my earthsuit
functions as it should—
I can feel it coming
barometric pressure
behind my heart
heaviness nearby
and I wonder what
how and when?
never why

will I bear it well?

no prayers for specifics—
we're each given our share
I ask for insight and grace
sometimes on my knees
often snuggled in bed
and I pray, oh! I pray
for surrender

the leaving times

over
the horizon
now visible
marching

precious friends
in trouble   falls,
trembling, frail
bones, cancer
threats of leaving—
clearing space

some days   accepting
other days
as though I could
ward off death—
theirs and mine

days

she walks with me,
death
not chummy,
not yet
but her whispers float
like dandelion seeds,
light on the wind
occasionally tickling
my nose

she's my life coach
coaxing   *write now*
write what's true
I try
I do

everyday new

I'm learning to be who I am, over and over again.
—Doug von Koss

each morning
a new body
what is this aging?
how to be gracious
with these shifts
today, grumpy feet
tomorrow's new
riddle to solve

our world, where we
can't have it all,
I choose this—
wrinkling on the outside
softening inside
like a fig in its drying
I don't want
to live backward
into youth's beauty
and folly   instead
welcome old age
with its threads
of wisdom
and more kindness

breaking

My heart is broken; what do you recommend?
Break it some more. —Leonard Cohen

seven people
this year gone
my circle, smaller
more precious
in the breaking

there's privilege
in reaching old age
yet loss upon loss
confronts us

all comes to forfeit
that's the voyage
the gift of a body

maybe it grows
this willingness
to leave
when it's time
I suspect
it may be so

trees sway

leaves turn crimson
crinkle and fall
breezes flutter
bearing them away

I guzzle breath
it passes so fast
sweeping marrow
into marvel
stand in the dark
owls hoot me
back into my bones
for a blink

surrender

the colicky infant yields
to the long-braided child
sulky teen gives way

to the brisk, busy woman
she cedes to a bowed back
and wild egret hair

it's the way of things
achingly evident yet
the carnal body squirms

capitulates
yes, to all of it

of course, be brave
face the bully
care for the injured wren

but most of all
love one another
then, like Beowulf

we must yield
the leasehold
of our days

fall into astonishment

my son's wild curls
line a raven's nest
soft for baby birds,
a flight of doves
mill the soil for seed,
the mare knows
licks her newborn foal

as I age into
cronehood—bowed
with wizened skin
and spiky hair,
the path divides—
astonishment
or despair

I choose awe!
marvels everywhere

reflection

today the glass
reflects I'm old
came swift
so short the straw

I slow down
but time sprints
evening|morning
night|again   each
day a fingersnap
every blink a blessing
dark|lightdark|light
reminding

noting breath
feeling heart's
mostly steady beat
how long   how long

that kind

I don't want
that kind of old—
querulous, afraid,
and downed by loss
instead,
curious
rich heart
and ready smile

to imbibe this life
full tilt—
greet pain's knife,
aches and griefs
that rend

two role models,
both mid-nineties
teach me—
their lifelong friends
are gone, yet
they greet each day—
add in joy
I ask to be that way

the waiting times

every day an illness
or a leaving, so unlike
fifty years ago
celebrations, storks
gifts and births
now death lingers
against the street post
outside my friends'
homes, not in the shadows—
slouchy, bold
flicking an ash
waiting

no—with the snap
of a finger
I send him away
it's the Friend who waits
curious, playful
ready to ramble
happy to walk
us home
no hat
certainly no cartoon
smoke
trailing in air

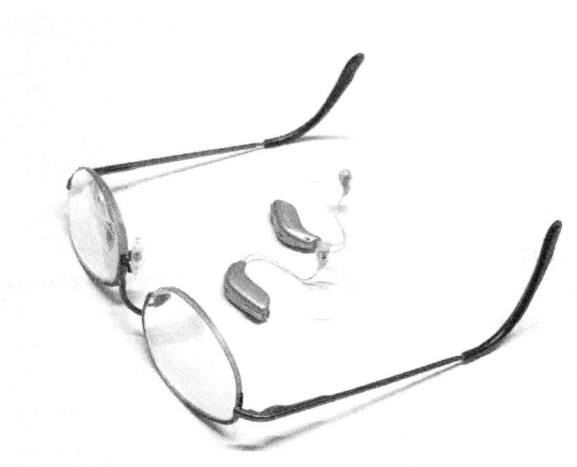

lifted

each morning
I am lifted
first light's glimmer
welcomes
my old body back

then lifted
by hearing aids
and trifocals
what magic!
chickadees come clear
their six-note call

most of all
lifted by love
I throw open the door
the breeze caresses
steady rain falls

give way

owl folds her wings
tucks her beak
into soft down
fox snuggles
next to her mate

I call into the dark
soft prayers
hear them filtered
by leaves, alighting
here and there

breathe chill air
promise of early light
the world, so still
alert for the engine
of morning

allow
it's getting late
now or
not now
always now

grace is here—
waiting for me
to open
give way
to the sacred embrace

good fortune

now past three-quarters
of a century
stiff hands, thinning hair
name retrieval
nouns wandering
so many
reasons to grouse—

I'm left with the grace
of verbs   they roam
or amble
coast through air
mimicking
change—pupa
into butterfly

we don't know what's
coming—
I float on those verbs
they ferry
me   teaching
letting go

laid spare

threadbare
with impending loss
burnished
worn through
rent and laid spare

that is how it is
on this tiny, spinning orb
pulled thin
stretched fine
translucent with grief

embodiment
exacts its price
undeniable,
I must face this
right now   right here

dancing the loss

every few months
a memo   sometimes
jar sometimes joy
demise
sliding my way

first light   autumn
bite invigorates
dog gambols
in the freshening

sugar maples' jewel
leaves ready to fall
I brighten too

past due

at the year of my birth
expected life span
seventy-two

already, seven
years past
shelf life
sell-by
best-before
or use-by

late bloomer
Mom used to say
to make me so

more than plugging
along   just
found my stride
my need
a decade of time

leaving it all
a villanelle

sometimes I long to simply take high flight
to leave this crooked world behind, alone
and reach in deep for purest, clearest light

it's madness here—the mean and righteous fight
they grab and push and nab the richest bone
sometimes I long to simply take high flight

and flee this place at dawn or plushest night
seek peace elsewhere, a place that is unknown
and reach in deep for purest, clearest light

to watch all suffering souls, their dreadful plight
it hurts my heart and makes me weighted stone
sometimes I long to simply take high flight

to soar, and bank, to find the broadest sight
and then unearth the place that's my true home
and reach in deep for purest, clearest light

how will I find the strength for loft and height
so courage, love, and beauty may atone?
sometimes I long to simply take high flight
and reach in deep for purest, clearest light

looking ahead

not the hospital
my prayer
bells, clangs
disinfectants   smells
despair

give me home
dule of doves feeding
fox   her delicate
tongue sipping
silence's blessing
and faithful dog
at my feet

the shift

in my ending season,
one minute
or twenty years
the work is clear
shifting from doing
to being—
my poem-a-day
doing, no doubt
but this doing
different,
slowed down
reflective
appropriate to
the season

I will write
until I cannot
praying
that day,
far off

the score

if I listen
with attentive care
behind sound
and into silence
it is here—
my inner song

not more nor less,
yet unlike yours—
every one of us
unique, each called
forth from being

when I study
the score,
entwining motifs
thread sections—
some minor
others major
the rising themes
more solace
more patience

what revelation
will the coda bring?

slow learner

in a nearby orchard
a choreography
of lichen-covered limbs

shaped by wind
by drought
and early pruning
her prime long gone
and fruit now falling
the apple
stands sentinel

now old, like the tree
bent and formed
by life's forces
I walk by you each day
my sister

borrowed

I am traceless
and faceless
filled with knowing
yet not known
walking the life
I was granted

called seeker
wife, mother
teacher, poet
old woman
I am none
of these

they are shawls
I slip on
and slip off
useful

I am breath
in a lifesuit
borrowed
for a while
before I must
give it back

the wish

as I get old
this wish grows strong

leave no truce
no name

no gravestone
nor place to be found

but in squirrel play
and billowing clouds

late light spilling
through birch on the hill

crickets and frogsong
the chorus at twilight

spring breezes touch
and the creek's steady fall

Acknowledgements

Many thanks to:

Fran Claggett-Holland for calling forth the poet in me

Peter Levitt for his steady reflection and feedback

Our skillful and attentive poetry critique group, **The Blue Moon Collective**—each poet is a gem. A heartfelt thank you!

Les Bernstein for the phrase "the ending season" and for putting her wise eyes on the manuscript before publication

Grant Chemidlin, my mentor at **PocketMFA**

Boudewijn Boom, my husband, special thanks and love for his support every day

Rupert Spira and **Elias Amidon**, teachers and friends who inform and deepen my life, and provided blurbs for the cover

Rosemerry Wahtola Trommer, for her friendship and blurb on the cover

Elias Amidon for the phrase "love and dust," and the title phrase "bewilderment and tenacity"

John Roedel for the phrase "skin-and-bone rollercoaster"

"in the road" was first published by the *New English Review*

"the welcome" was first published by *Chiron Review* with the title "unknown"

"leaving it all" was first published by *The Penwood Review*

"the wish" was first published in *One Day*, Redwood Writers 2024 poetry anthology

Amrita Skye Blaine develops themes of aging, disability, and awakening. She received an MFA in Creative Writing from Antioch University in 2003, and a PocketMFA in poetry in 2024. She has published a memoir, a three-novel trilogy, and has been featured in fifteen anthologies including ten poetry anthologies.

She has been writing poetry steadily since she turned seventy, and for the last two-and-a-half years, has been writing a poem every day.

Her poems have been accepted by *Heart Balm, Soul-Lit, Braided Way Magazine, The Merton Seasonal, The Penwood Review, Poetry Breakfast, Delta Poetry Review,* the *New English Review, Chiron Review, Amethyst Review, One Art,* and *Blue Heron Review.* Her next book of poetry, *every riven thing,* will be released mid-2025 by Finishing Line Press.

Websites and contact information:
    www.theheartofthematter-dailyreminders.org
    www.skyeblaine.com
    amritaskyepoetry@gmail.com

Made in the USA
Monee, IL
08 March 2025

13692791R00059